Coaching Your Way to
SUCCESS

Joe.
It's Time, To
ACHIEVE MORE !!
I BELIEVE IN You!!

50 Tips For Achieving Success In All Areas Of Your Life

Britt "Coach" Davenport #1

Brett M. Davenport

Published by Empire Financial Network, Inc.

Printed in the United States of America

Davenport, Brett M.
    Coaching Your Way to Success, 50 Tips For Achieving Success In All Areas Of Your Life / by Brett M. Davenport

Library of Congress Cataloging-in-Publication Data
    ISBN: 978-0-578-05565-7

Cover/Interior Design by: Dawn Teagarden
Dawnteagarden@embarqmail.com

Warning – Disclaimer
The purpose of this book is to educate and entertain. The author or publisher does not guarantee that anyone following the techniques, suggestions, tips, ideas, or strategies will become successful. The author and publisher shall have neither liability nor responsibility to anyone with respect to any loss or damage caused, or alleged to be caused, directly or indirectly by the information contained in this book.

DEDICATION

This book is dedicated to my beautiful bride, Joanne for her unconditional love, warm smile, that remarkable sparkle of hope that resides within her eyes, unwavering dedication to family and her charming personality. I cherish everyday as we walk hand in hand through life's wonderful maze of opportunity. I love you Sweetheart!

Our two boys Harrison and Connor who make me proud in the way they respond to each success and every failed attempt. You are gifted leaders with very bright futures. Always keep your smile and your positive "I CAN" attitudes. I'm the luckiest Dad in the world!

My mother (Nancy) who has always been our families' pillar of strength; she reminds us often to stop and smell the roses along the path of success. Thank you for all you have done and continue to do!

My father (Vern) who taught me to be generous to the less fortunate, focus on my inner strength and that anything is possible. Just go do it!

My late mother-in-law, mom (Fannie) who I miss very much and think of daily; you're the tops!

My father-in-law, dad (Dick) all the great times we have had on and off the golf course. I enjoy being your co-pilot and admire your free spirit!

To my brothers and sisters, brothers and sisters In-law thank you for your support, all the fun times and I believe the best is yet to come!

A special thank you goes out to my grandparents for always being there for me, passing words of wisdom and knowing you will be forever my guiding light!

My extended family and so many wonderful friends that it would take pages to recognize, please know I feel blessed to have you in my life!

With all my love!

ACKNOWLEDGEMENTS

This book covers over 4 decades of my current personal philosophy regarding the idea that we CAN do more, be more, give more, learn more, enjoy more and that anything is POSSIBLE!

Giving full and proper recognition to all those whose actions, thoughts and words have influenced my own, is difficult, but a handful of individuals so deeply touched me that I must acknowledge their contribution as friends, as business associates, and as mentors or individuals.

To my dear friend and mentor, Jack "the great one" Kinder, who inspired me to become the best leader I could possibly be by positively influencing the lives of others. He challenged me to become a Dale Carnegie graduate when I felt like I had no more time to give. He taught me the value of vision, goal setting and to always believe in yourself. He gave me the power within myself to understand that readers are leaders and that education never stops. I will forever be grateful!

To my dear friend Mr. Peter Ferguson, who gave me my first professional opportunity in the financial Services industry where I have enjoyed 22 years. In-addition he took a chance on a young individual with little resume experience and promoted me into management where I have been for more than 20 years. Your words of encouragement and high expectations will forever be my personal measuring stick and you will always be my Rock of Gibraltar!

To my dear friend and business associate, Mr. Mike Cataldo, who's the most proficient executive I have had the opportunity to work with. You are a genius marketer with brilliant business acumen. I have cultivated many lessons which have made me a more effective executive and business owner. What I have enjoyed most about our relationship is the staunch family man that you are!

To my dear friend Mr. Louis Olerio, who in my opinion represents leadership to the highest degree. Your charismatic personality and attention to detail influenced me as a young leader more than you will ever know. I admire your consistent ability to always see good and thrive in the face of adversity. Thank you for guiding me to the infamous high road!

To my current coach, James Malinchak, for always challenging me to do more and get out of my comfort zone. I appreciate your words of wisdom and look forward to the future!

To my dear friend and mentor, the late Joseph "one more round" Carucci; in my 46 years I can say with complete convictions that I have never seen a person more committed and generous to their community than Joe Carucci. Joe demonstrated that we all have a choice every day to let things happen; or Joe's way, to take charge and make things happen. I will never forget the adventure we shared in creating the "KNOTHOLE GANG" , how many kids we inspired and the life long strategic partnerships that were developed from one executed idea! I will miss you, our conversations and your mentorship, but be certain I will carry your torch forever!

WHAT OTHERS ARE SAYING ABOUT BRETT M. DAVENPORT...

"Simply, Brett Davenport is the most Positive, Passionate, Honest and Intelligent Leader (in every sense of the word) I have ever met!!!!"

> – *Ross Kraft, LUTCF*
> *President, Meridian Group of New York, Inc.*

"Nobody's going to just show up with a trophy, with all the hard work done, and put your name on it.

In other-words, nobody is going to just give you that beautiful house and car, the country club membership, the solid, stable and meaningful relationships with your spouse, children and friends....you have to **learn how to overcome the fear** and do the hard work, balancing your time, talent and resources in life to achieve the goals you want. This is what Brett has taught me to do.

With Brett, at first it's about goal setting and getting focused and motivated on completing tasks to reach a goal....but over time, it become less about the goal and more about the soul...more about life and less about strife. The result is the ability to see past the fear of failure (career, family, relationships) by learning the necessary skills and techniques to achieve one's goals in life. Then it's just a matter of applying those skills to the goals of your journey in life, no matter what you do.

Learning this from Brett has yielded results, period! I have gone from cold calling in the insurance business to being a Founding Partner in a Wealth Management Investment Firm, happily married with 2 wonderful children, and having a real sense of well-being in my life."

> – *Michael G. Edwards, CIMA, CRPC*
> *Founder & Partner of Strategic Wealth Partners, LLC*

"Brett Davenport has been an integral aspect of my professional development. Not only has he been a guiding force in my own personal achievements, but he has given me the tools and resources to succeed in the business world. Brett's willingness to help the eager individuals that serve him is a true testament to his knowledge of what it takes to build a leader and the secret to surrounding yourself with other successful, driven professionals. He is one of the most inspirational people in the business world today. Be sure to listen when he takes the time to give you advice and encouragement, it will make the difference! Believe."

— *Ashley Hoey, PR & Marketing, Maloney & Fox, New York, NY*

"Brett Davenport is an incredibly insightful leader in our industry. He is a no-nonsense mind who understands the profession, its challenges and unbridled opportunities. This is an impressive individual who is as candid as he is imaginative."

— *Laurence Barton, PhD, President and O. Alfred Granum Professor of Management, The American College*

"I have the utmost respect for Brett Davenport. He inspires you the moment he says "hello" - if you're looking for an individual to motivate, Brett Davenport is your guy. Having known and worked with Brett for the better part of 10 years - I have never seen a down moment. His message is inspiring, as is the way he carries himself in his professional and family life."

— *Gary Hoy , CEO, Appointment University*

"Brett Davenport repeatedly participated in learning with an extremely positive attitude and open mind. He is eager to learn everything he can to further develop and polish his skills and abilities. Brett also became a fantastic role model for others in his course. His ability to interact with people effectively, communicate his ideas passionately, and handle himself as a professional under extreme pressure are just a few of the qualities Brett demonstrated on a consistent basis. We admired his passion for life and learning as well as his empathy for others. As a leader, Brett is someone that I would definitely enjoy working for and would also feel very comfortable referring to any business looking for an integral team member."

— *Leslie English, Managing Partner, Dale Carnegie*

"Brett Davenport is an outstanding student of leadership. A quick examination of his professional career path clearly illustrates his leadership and how others have recognized his leadership capabilities. He has the ability to inspire others to perform well beyond their expectations. Brett is a team player and major contributor to the team."

> *– Glenn Boseman, DBA, CLU, CLF, Professor of Leadership*
> *The American College*

"Two words to describe my friend and mentor Brett Davenport... Infectious SUCCESS!!!! He embodies the words positive energy and is my living, go to and learn from empowerment manual. Brett's clear, concise, relative and just plain effective leadership has molded my personal and professional dreams into reality. Bottom line, if you are privileged to be mentored by Brett Davenport you will leave a better person from the first conversation. He resonates leadership from his core. Brett is simply the best in the business!"

> *– Corey (Coach) Parker, President of Strength in Motion*
> *Former Syracuse University Associate Head Strength and*
> *Conditioning Football Coach*

"It is said that, "A great leader is someone people choose to follow to places that they wouldn't go themselves." Brett Davenport is such a leader and motivator. He creates an environment where people feel energized and capable of accomplishing anything. He leads as a partner in the effort while creating a feeling of empowerment in the people whose lives he touches. I am proud to call Brett Davenport a friend."

> *– Peter Molnar, President & CEO, Molnar Financial Group, Inc.*

"In the 23 years that I have worked with Brett he has shown himself to be a great coach, motivator and leader. His indefatigable passion and ability to take the most challenging situation and break the solution down into small achievable actions is how Brett leads others to success. I can tell you from personal experience whether it is on the football field, the golf course or in the boardroom you want Brett Davenport on your team."

> *– Christopher Mee*
> *President, Financial Planning Channel Wood Logan*
> *John Hancock Annuities*

"I have had the pleasure of knowing and working with Brett Davenport for over 10 years. Brett is family-oriented, civic minded, focused, and results driven. His enthusiasm is contagious, and he is an immediate asset in any environment. In sum, Brett Davenport is the *"real deal."*

— *Raymond Quick, Educator / Consultant*

"Brett Davenport gave me a shot at a promotion as a young man when others may not have and I am forever grateful. He saw something in me that others, including myself, could not see. That was the tip of the iceberg. What he gave me thereafter was an education in life, leadership, and management. Always the consummate coach, Brett was able to elevate me to levels I would not have risen to on my own. This was to lay the foundation for my development for years to come. I still, to this day, go back to the techniques and guidance that Brett has given me over the years. Brett personified passion, desire, professionalism, and getting the most out of individuals. I consider Brett a lifelong Mentor, Coach, and Friend."

— *Matt Dauksza, CFP, CLU*
Trophy Winning, Manager of Financial Services

"Not everyone is a winner, and not everyone is a part of a winning team. It's not always easy to win; winning takes specific qualities that special people possess. Being energetic and having a dynamic personality filled with passion and determination are the keys to the winning attitude. Brett Davenport has the unique ability to consistently demonstrate the qualities of a winner, and more importantly, he has the ability to get people to emulate him. A winner isn't always a great leader, but a great leader is always a winner. In Brett's case, he is a great leader that always wins! I have had the pleasure of working with Brett, and at no point in my life have I been more challenged, motivated, excited and determined to succeed. I am amazed at his ability to get people to action, and impressed that he can motivate an entire team to the same vision. A great leader has the skill of finding a person's strengths and teaching him or her to recognize their own winning capabilities. It is this skill of uncovering talent that makes Brett so valuable. His consistent coaching and mentoring is my personal roadmap to future successes and victories."

— *Lucas Gross,*
Award Winning Sales Manager & Personal Trainer

"As a recurring Top of the Table and Million Dollar Round Table producer in the Life Insurance Industry, I have had the opportunity and good fortune to be in the presence of some of the world's top motivational speakers. Brett Davenport, during the time that we were associates, not only recruited and developed some of the most successful Life Insurance agents and sales managers, but succeeded in maintaining a high level of energetic motivation for his entire staff. Through his positive management style and winning outlook, he led his team to win his company's National Trophy for Life Insurance sales. He truly ranks among the world's best!"

> – *Dalton J. Raymond, 14 time qualifier for the prestigious MDRT "Top of the Table", Trophy Winning Insurance Professional, multiple times with multiple companies*

"Brett Davenport is the most professional, motivating, powerful leader and coach I have ever met! Over the years he has taught me so much that it feels like I utilize something from his tool box of wisdom every day! His smile, positive attitude and high level of energy are extremely rare and always leave you feeling better about yourself when you're in his presence! I'm proud to call Brett my Mentor!"

> – *Mark Spinelli, Manager, Quiznos Restaurant Full-Time College Student*

"If you happen to be one of those fortunate people in life who has someone come into your life, extend a sincere hand of friendship, mutual respect, and devotes his boundless energy to learning how to "coach" you to the best you can be and show you how, just maybe, your expectations have been limited by your own fear of stepping out of your comfort zone....a man who has passion, conviction and extraordinary skills in persuasion, motivation and public speaking ...a man who loves life and cherishes every blessing he has received...then, let me introduce you to Brett Davenport!"

> – *Lee M. Gatta, MS, CLU, AEP, ChFC Financial Planner and 9 time "MDRT" Qualifier*

"Brett Davenport has not only been a great friend but a person who has influenced me both physically and mentally. As a motivator and leader his beliefs and actions have helped me to become one of the top sales representatives within my company. My work ethic would not be where it is today without the persistence and focus that Brett has taught me. The tips that he has in his book truly can change your life if you believe in yourself and him."

> – *Adam Gillan, Award Winning, Customer Business Development Manager, Pharmaceuticals*

"Brett Davenport's presence alone is motivating. When Brett speaks, you know you are listening to a person who understands how to identify a goal, reach it, and enjoy the process. Brett's energy is focused, powerful, and inspiring. He has succeeded in multiple venues— including business and education— and amazingly, he is genuinely interested in serving others and helping them achieve their dreams. If you have the opportunity to hear him speak, treat yourself. You will be moved out of your seat and higher on your path."

— Julie Gedro, MBA, PHR, EdD, Associate Professor of Business, Management & Economics, Director, FORUM Central Faculty Chair, Empire State College

"Brett Davenport is the most passionate and motivational speaker on leadership in the business today! Brett's personal coaching changed my life. To have passion and purpose in your career, in your education and in your life is the core essence of Brett's mentoring. Five years into a mediocre career in the financial services industry, I had the privilege of being recruited, working for and being mentored by one of the finest leaders in America, Brett Davenport! Although I was motivated, I lacked focus and direction; Brett changed that and took me to levels I did not believe were possible through proper goal setting and vision! There is no question in my mind that his coaching has been and will continuously influence my life in a positive direction!"

— Joseph Basile CRPC®, CLU®, ChFC®
Assistant Vice President and Senior Financial Advisor
Merrill Lynch

"Leadership: Merriam-Webster defines it as; an act or instance of leading. I however, expand their definition to include; one's ability to consistently lead others to perform beyond their expectations. Brett M. Davenport exemplifies my definition of Leadership.

As a Husband, Father, Colleague, Friend, and Coach, Brett Davenport has successfully led individuals and organizations to heights otherwise not achievable. It's been my experience that Brett's formula of applying concepts of positive thinking, determination, and commitment to **"Team"** are the foundation of his result-based success.

It is my privilege to be his Brother, Friend, and Student."

— Brent L. Davenport, Managing Principal
Infrastructure Design, Inc

"Study the past,
Live the moment,
Plan the future."

–*Brett (Coach) Davenport*

CONTENT

COMMUNICATION IS ANY RELATIONSHIP'S HEARTBEAT

Mastering the Art of Understanding

Communication problems have arisen from antiquated methods of connection: the pony express, the telegraph, the switchboard. Likewise, fuzzy CB transmissions, tin cans with string, and notes passed in class have been met with puzzled, "Huhs?"

One might wonder if in this, the communication age, with all of the emails, texts, and public messages floating through cyberspace, if we

---

haven't once again fallen into the trap of, "Huh?" We might also wonder if we focus too intently on communication in all of its methods, rather than in its primary purpose and benefit.

Superficially, communication can be described as broadcasting, where it is assumed that the receiver is understanding; or, sadly, a shallow exchange of information might also be considered "communication," when it's actually just a conversation. But real communication, with substance, genuine exchange, empathy, and intimacy, is communication that results in *understanding*.

Within a quality communication, three indispensable components will be found: listening, personal revelation, and feedback. Does your coach know that you're struggling with self-confidence? Does your employee know that you're struggling with his lack of performance? Does your child know that you're struggling with her recent behavior? Could mutual understanding be the answer?

Most everyone can describe communication on paper, but the real thing takes practice and determination. Exercise your abilities by listening intently, asking probing questions, offering constructive feedback, and prudently revealing parts of yourself that contribute to understanding. In turn, do what's necessary to appreciate the views of other participants, because until that can be accomplished, the heart of matters will never be grasped; nor will matters of heart.

> ## "The single biggest problem in communication is the illusion that it has taken place."
> ### –*George Bernard Shaw*

"PLEASE" AND "THANK-YOU" WILL NEVER GO OUT OF STYLE

Stand Out with Gracious Measures

Are you offended when someone shuts a door in your face? Or when you personally deliver the quarterly report to your boss and he can't even say *thank-you*? Or how about when someone *tells* you to move, without a simple *please*?

Firstly, don't allow the negative feelings that this rude behavior conveys to creep into your persona. The worst way that you can deal with rude behavior is to respond with rudeness. Instead, use the opportunity to set an example with your own polite mannerisms.

And secondly, use rude behavior as an example of how you choose not to act. Instead, be generous with your politeness. Use *please* every time a situation allows for it. Use *thank-you* copiously; even to thank people in unexpected ways – for things like criticism, or canceling a meeting with plenty of time to spare, or for allowing you to lose graciously.

Politeness grabs the attention of leaders. Kind words and actions are outward signs of your inward appreciation and respect.

Good manners show respect, and in turn, demand respect for you. When you use good manners, it makes it clear that you are considerate of others' feelings, and that putting people at ease is important to you.

Good manners are nothing more than manifestations of the Golden Rule. Be polite to others, as you would want others to be polite to you.

"Good manners will open doors that the best education cannot."
–*Clarence Thomas*

START WITH
THE END IN MIND

Successful Individuals, Teams, and Organizations do

Where are you going? If you don't know, how can you expect to get there?

What is your purpose? If you don't know, how can you expect to accomplish it?

Often, businesses and other organizations will post a mission statement, in order to establish a goal, a horizon, or a destination.

Like an artist who sets up camp just east of a spectacular mountain view, you should have a clear picture of where your journey will end.

When that artist picks up his brush and arranges his paints, he feels confident that he has the tools that will aid him in accomplishing his goal. When you name principles, or truths, that are intrinsic to your key goal, you also have the tools with which to arrive at your goal.

From the artist's first brush stroke to his last finishing touch, he is confident in his ability to arrive at the scene that lies before him. You too, can establish a scene, or credo, as vivid as the artist's. You can gather the tools that you need and accomplish your goal, all with that vision entrenched in your everyday activities.

Put your mission, or end story, in writing. Make it the compass that guides you in your daily activities. Return to it for inspiration when you feel that you're falling off course. Admire its stoic nature – for it is an inflexible nucleus, immune to external changes that might otherwise obscure the prize from your eye.

> ## "If you don't know where you are going, you will probably end up somewhere else."
> ### *–Lawrence J. Peter*

WHAT YOU DO SPEAKS SO LOUDLY, I CAN'T HEAR WHAT YOU SAY

Why Actions Trump Words

Rhetoric was once a deeply studied and highly respected art of discourse. A central method for proving points and furthering arguments, rhetoric captivated philosophers as renowned as Plato and Aristotle.

But in today's world, rhetoric's classification has sunk to that of insult. Its modern definition is simply "persuasive language." It has lost its connection to knowledge and intent.

So why has rhetoric come to be synonymous with empty words? Because the actions of the speaker, whether committed simultaneously or after the fact, have proven to speak louder than any linguistic expression.

If a preacher speaks uplifting words while wringing her hands, blinking rapidly, and sweeping sweat from her brow, does she really believe what she's saying? The answer is *no*. Listen to a speaker's recorded words and you will gather less information about that person than you would by watching video with the volume turned off. Non-verbal cues account for 93 percent of all communication.

If a friend invites you out for a meal, but has failed to show up for your last two meetings, will you trust that you'll have company for dinner? You might want to count on take-out for one. All of us have had enough experience with empty words to know that the best determining factor of expected behavior is previous behavior.

Don't commit rhetoric. Past and present action trumps present and future words. Always keep this in the forefront of your mind. Speeches can be written to say anything, but actions continue to say everything.

"Ironically, making a statement with words is the least effective method."
–Grey Livingston

UNDER-PROMISE AND OVER-DELIVER – A WINNING STRATEGY

"Cross my heart and hope to die." This statement may be meant to quell fears; but how effective is it, considering that one well-intentioned, but broken, promise can cast a dark shadow over a personal or business relationship for a lifetime?

Psychologists tell us that in situations tainted with uncertainty, we naturally look to those who are more certain of that situation for information that can help us to set expectations. Without expectations, we feel helpless…vulnerable – we cling to them, because often, they are the closest we can come to truth.

When expectations, or promises, are not fulfilled, we feel disappointed. When we think of the trust that we invested in the promise-breaker, we feel betrayed, duped, taken advantage of.

But to the contrary, when our expectations are exceeded, we feel like we've scored dividends beyond our investments. We see our expectation source as an expert who can be trusted, and whose credibility and conviction stand taller than any rhetoric.

You know the sting of betrayal. And because you do, you hold the power to exceed every expectation that is placed on you. Every time that you deliver a more fulfilling experience than was expected, you create spontaneous satisfaction.

You have the power to use promises in one of two ways: You can *under-promise*, or you can be crushed *under* the weight of a *promise* that you cannot keep.

Resolve to never again cross your heart. Instead, put your heart into delivering your best possible performance.

"Well done is better than well said."
–*Benjamin Franklin*

ASK QUESTIONS –
VERY FEW PEOPLE
ARE MIND READERS

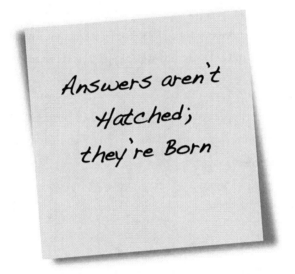

Answers aren't
Hatched;
they're Born

Answers are the fuel that you need to further your personal development and to achieve personal success. But from where do they come? Do they emerge from an inanimate shell? Or are they born from a living, breathing being with the power to bring them into the world?

Are you ready to acknowledge that you have the power to supply your life with the answers it needs to advance? Are you ready to flex that power by asking questions?

When you pipe up and ask questions (of others) that are unique to your purpose, you spark a metamorphosis in the mind, and on the mouth, of the questioned person. When he or she must tailor the knowledge that they already hold to fit the format or purpose of your question, you are automatically presented with a customized answer – to serve as fuel for your particular purpose.

Without the question mark, the acquiring of targeted knowledge would be out of the question. Pieces of general information would drift aimlessly, never really hitting the mark for any of our unique purposes. Additionally, without the precious question, great thinkers would have never established the norms under which we operate.

Don't waste time pining for answers to questions that you are fearful of asking. Instead, make your own question "mark." Mark yourself as focused, curious, willing to learn, desirous of betterment, and best of all – the one from whom your very own, personalized answers are born.

"He who asks is a fool for five minutes, but he who does not ask remains a fool forever."
–Chinese Proverb

ACCOUNTABILITY IS A GOOD THING,

if you Want to Get Ahead

Accountability is no longer a dirty word – provided that you can adopt it as an asset; learn to view it as a powerful tool in your quest for success. Personal accountability equates to trust, respect, and forward motion – both for you and for those affected by your efforts.

Accountability didn't earn its own bad reputation. Instead, it was assigned a scarlet letter by bad management, as an idea that its only place is under a micromanaging leader who intimidates and imposes a sense of professional obligation. To the contrary, when personal accountability is viewed and used correctly, it can be a constructive concept that works to push people toward betterment.

When you set appropriate and challenging goals for yourself, the highest power that you can possibly answer to is yourself. When you expect certain behavior from yourself, and practice accountability to yourself, you will be moved to satisfy your toughest customer – you.

Few of us will ever feel responsible to an outside source for the amount of time that it takes to realize success. When you hold yourself accountable for your choices, you make better future choices, and propel yourself from stagnant waters and into a river of progress.

Remember: it's not *your* motivation or *your* success if you're not accountable to your highest power. Personal accountability gives you power over your own life, because it holds responsible the most powerful person in your life – You.

Be your own highest power. When you hold yourself accountable, you will be counted.

> ## "Accountability breeds response-ability."
> *–Stephen R. Covey*

GOAL-SETTING SOUNDS EASY, AND IT IS WITH A COACH

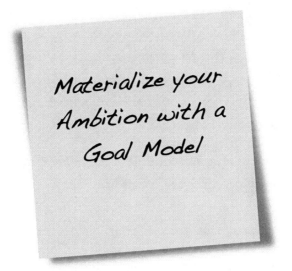

Materialize your Ambition with a Goal Model

Look to someone who exhibits the same type of personal success that you desire, and you'll find an individual who has already set and achieved the same goals that you're contemplating.

You need a goal model. Just as important as the business plan is to the entrepreneur, or the playbook is to the football coach, or the to-do-list is to the homemaker, the goal model is an indispensable resource for anyone striving for betterment.

A goal model is an imitation-worthy expert who has set and achieved goals in the pursuit of the same achievements that you hope to achieve for yourself. Unlike a role model (someone whose achievements you might admire), a goal model is someone whose approach and determination you admire; someone whose entire journey is worth chronicling.

Goal models demand accountability. A personal choice, accountability is an incredibly effective form of motivation. If a goal model is invited into the goal-setting process, the apprentice goal-setter will not only be driven by his or her own subconscious, but by a figure to whom that apprentice feels accountable.

Motivation, like many other internal dialogues, is obscure. But if it were to come to life, it might materialize in the form of a coach, a teacher, or other goal model. With a goal model, motivation is no longer an intangible or discountable commodity.

Bring your goals to authentic life – with a living, breathing goal model.

> ## "The most important single influence in the life of a person is another person…who is worthy of emulation."
> *–Paul D. Shafer*

WHERE IS YOUR BULL'S-EYE?

Focusing with Precision

An archer focuses on the bull's-eye of his target. He doesn't aspire for his arrow to land anywhere within the outer rings of the target, so why would he settle for anything less than a bull's-eye? Likewise, if the archer misses the bull's-eye, he doesn't stroll leisurely to the sight of the target and adjust the bull's-eye to rest where his arrow has landed. He reaches into his quiver, grasps another arrow, and

---

intensifies his focus on his only acceptable goal – dead center.

Your commitment to, and your focus on, your goal cannot be genuine if it possesses an evolutionary quality. If your goal changes every time your focus changes, you will be shooting at a zigzagging target – nearly impossible to hit.

Your goal is your rock; the mainstay onto which your attention must be directed.

Maintaining focus isn't always easy. Often, finding a mentor, study group, parenting group, or coach is necessary. Just as the sights on the archer's bow help him to concentrate on the bull's-eye, external motivators can be invaluable to you in remaining focused.

The magnitude of your goal is not as important as the focus that you view it with. If you need to start with easy targets (ones that are large, easy to hit, and within close range), do that. And as your focusing skills increase, you can increase the intensity of your goals – move those targets farther down the range, so that you may move closer to the benefits that they offer.

"If you're going to hunt elephants, don't get off the trail for a rabbit."
–T. Boone Pickens

FAILURE IS TRULY AN OPPORTUNITY TO DO BETTER

Giving yourself the Freedom to Fail

Though on the surface, it might seem counterintuitive, you must demand failure of yourself. Unless you're willing to try things that might fail, you will never arrive at the success you dream of.

Maybe you aspire to be a concert pianist. You have the skills, you've worked hard, but now you need to put your talent out there for the world to see. You've made a list of thirty different avenues. Some involve finding an agent, others involve direct auditions for productions, and others involve a variety of marketing attempts. You know that some methods will fail. What you may not have considered is that with every failure, you move closer to success. With your first disappointment, you will have narrowed your list to twenty-nine, then twenty-eight, and so on...until you narrow your list to the one or two methods that might work.

Because you know that trying may result in failure, be prepared for it. Have a plan in place to review the happenings and to extract pieces of learning.

Too often, we believe that if we fail once, we, ourselves, are failures. That couldn't be more incorrect. There's only one thing that can deem you a failure – to stop trying. When you are disappointed and surrender your goals, *you* fail.

Give yourself the freedom to fail through experimentation and exploration. Welcome each one for what it is: a scholarship for advancement to the next level. When you do, you'll guarantee your forward progress.

> ## "Failure is simply the opportunity to begin again, this time more intelligently."
> ### –Henry Ford

TODAY IS A GAME CHANGER

Tapping into the Power of NOW

"There will always be tomorrow." That's a trap that the unsuccessful fall into. Sure, excluding your last day, there will always be a tomorrow. But if you keep vowing to start to change your life tomorrow, your tomorrows will amass into yesterdays…a long, crumpled trail of empty yesterdays.

You might have to plan ahead for the season play-offs, or a birthday party, or a tri-state conference. But to change the direction of your life, the best time to start is now.

If you were to compare your life to a baseball game, you might feel as though you've been striking out – not able to see the curve balls, or feeling too sluggish to keep up with the fast balls. Maybe the sun has been in your eyes, or the wind has been pushing against you, making it difficult to catch the fly balls.

Don't lose hope. You have this day, and that alone is reason to try. It's only the third inning, at best. You're in the game, and there's still plenty of time to turn your RBI record on its head – if you start today.

Today is filled with possibility. You have 1,440 minutes to spend as you wish. You can make the phone calls, schedule the meetings, put in the practice time, hug your kids, write a letter that's been overdue – because today is your springboard, your birth to the rest of life, the inning in which the crack of the bat will signal the turn-around of the entire game.

> "Time is limited, so I better wake up every morning fresh and know that I have just one chance to live this particular day right, and to string my days together into a life of action, and purpose."
>
> –*Lance Armstrong*

BE BRILLIANT AT THE BASICS

Mastering your Craft = Stability for Ambitions

A young man mixed mortar for master craftsmen who stacked bricks, blocks, and stones. He watched closely; admired their skills. Years later, he was adopted as an apprentice. His young hands worked alongside pairs of old ones, mimicking their dexterity. He learned to stack stones so that they fit like puzzle pieces.

Years later, he skillfully built his own artistically precise creations. He had become a master mason, famous for his stable structures.

Decades after the start of his career, the mason felt that it was time for a change, so he worked as an apprentice to a master builder, in order to learn the complexities of carpentry. By the time he was ready to build his own house, the man was a master at masonry and a competent study in carpentry. The foundation of his home was stacked with professional capability – the rest with competency.

Because the foundation of a structure supports the rest of the building, it is imperative that it be strong and capable. When you support ambition with well-developed basic skills, you can promote higher success at greater levels.

When anything is said to be failing, we don't hear that the figurative roof is leaking. Instead, we hear that the foundation of the system is crumbling.

To move on to larger ambitions, you must master the skills that build the basis of your discipline. Repairs can be made to anything above the foundation; but weak groundwork leaves the builder holding a toolbox filled with ineffective tools.

> ## "Because if you have a strong foundation like we have, then you can build or rebuild anything on it. But if you've got a weak foundation you can't build anything."
> ### –Jack Scalia

A POSITIVE ATTITUDE IS WORTH CATCHING!

It's an Inspiration Infection

Like an anti-viral hand-washing poster hung in the middle school hallway, when you don a positive attitude, you become a billboard plastered with a list of optimism's benefits.

When you anticipate that the best will happen, you empower yourself to make the best happen. Those who are fortunate enough to witness this phenomenon will catch your bug. They will want to jump on… to join in the evident benefits of your positive attitude.

Attitudes mill around us everyday. There are the negative ones, which seek out the worst and use those findings to confirm that the world "really is a rotten place." And then there are those that flutter about, lighter than air, affirming the good that exists in the world. Their commonality? They are both more infectious than any media-televised influenza outbreak.

When you surround yourself with positive-thinking people, you will barely be able to avoid becoming infected. You'll immediately notice that they have realized success, that they are alive with energy, that they possess the power to make things happen, that they are respected, and that they are indisputably inspirational.

A game plan for your attitude reformation? Surround yourself with those who are most obviously infected with the positive bug. Read the words of those who are notoriously positive. Intentionally place yourself in situations in which smiles are inevitable. And finally, visualize success – because with a positive attitude, you need only believe to achieve.

Turn on your light and you will dispel darkness. The laws of physics demand it.

> ## "The person who sends out positive thoughts activates the world around him positively and draws back to himself positive results."
> *–Norman Vincent Peale*

WHEN THE WILL TO BELIEVE YOU CAN IS STRONGER THAN FEAR,

You Create your Own Good Fortune

Fortune telling is significantly popular, particularly in certain social groups. The attraction lies in the perception that the receiver of the divine information is gaining self-understanding that will lead to increased personal power – which will in turn, lead to success in many areas of life.

The intellect behind fortune telling is this: many statements made by the clairvoyant are statements that can apply to a vast majority of the public, are subjective (depending on the conception by the receiver), or are so flatteringly positive that the receiver wants to believe the soothsayer's prophecies.

Whether or not you choose to believe in fortune telling, there is much to be learned from this practice. When we are given reason to believe that we can accomplish something, we are staggeringly more apt to achieve our goals. When a "certainty" is established, fear is no longer a driving (or stagnant) force in our decision-making.

The secret to gaining this power without the crystal ball or tarot cards is to place faith in your own assessments of self. Tell yourself that you see a promotion in your future, and you will increase your confidence and your chances of success. Tell yourself that you have no chance of landing the puck in the goal, and you'll save the goalie lots of effort.

You don't have to rely on the stars to invent your fortune, and fear is never stronger than any positive self-perception of ability. By simply saying, "I can," you create your own fortune.

"Expect to Win"
–Brett (Coach) Davenport

PERSISTENCY – IT TAKES A LONG TIME TO GROW OLD FRIENDS

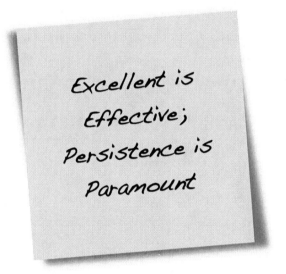

Excellent is Effective; Persistence is Paramount

It's an old girl scout mantra: *Make new friends, keep the old. One is silver, and the other gold.*

New friends are certainly valuable, but more valuable are time-tested relationships – the ones built through determination, diligence, and the awareness that to be excellent is effective, but to be persistent is paramount.

In order to illustrate this point, I'd like to suggest that you adopt this metaphor: excellence, talent, ability…they are the new friend, the silver coin, the semi-precious commodity. A tireless work ethic, a commitment to sharing your talents, an inability to accept failure… they are the old friend, the gold coin, the uber-precious metal.

Persistency is accomplished when you commit to doing "your thing" well and without limit. Employers, coaches, and talent scouts are often hesitant to hire, recruit, or contract with a tenderfoot – not because that person doesn't show exceptional talent, but because he or she hasn't yet had the opportunity to prove that they have commitment to their craft.

You will know that you have accomplished persistency when it no longer feels like persistency. When others recognize your diligence as an asset, you can then claim experience.

As cliché as it may sound, don't give up. Be your very own success tycoon: collect a modest number of silver coins, but instead of adding more silver to your bank, work on industriously investing that silver – until you can claim a collection of solid gold.

> ## "So many individuals, teams, organizations, families give up, not realizing just how close they were to success."
> *–Brett (Coach) Davenport*

DON'T PUT OFF UNTIL TOMORROW WHAT CAN BE ACCOMPLISHED TODAY

The Procrastination Trap

Think of all the things you need to do right now. Now imagine that each task is an article of soiled clothing.

It's easy to put off doing laundry until tomorrow – you've got plenty of clothing in your closet, you've got socks and underwear in the drawer, and it would make more sense to dedicate one solid block of time to doing laundry, right? After all, the manufacturer recommends doing only full loads. And, oh yes, electricity rates drop after six o'clock p.m., so it would make perfect sense to wait until an evening when you'll be at home…which would be…next Tuesday…barring any last-minute dinner plans.

When you procrastinate, you not only waste time reasoning your way out of work that might only take a fraction of the time, but you add to the mental weight that you bear. Instead of a few important tasks lying ahead of you, there is a mountain of tasks lying behind you, often just out of your reach.

Opportunity doesn't announce itself, nor does it reign itself according to your procrastination "schedule." What if you're called for a last-minute job interview? And all of your pants are buried in the laundry pile?

Remember that when you put things off until tomorrow, the chances of them getting done tomorrow are remote. The chances of you never being caught up are much greater. When you finally decide to tackle your task(s), your proverbial pile of laundry might be too large for any human to manage.

"Procrastination is opportunity's assassin."
–*Victor Kiam*

CHARACTER IS BEST DEMONSTRATED BY WHAT WE DO...

When no one is watching

Life is like a movie. Lots of us have two characters: the one that's on-screen (the character that is played), and the one that's off-screen (the character that is).

So who are you when you're alone? Are you the same person at the wrestling match, the poker game, and Sunday mass? Or have you adopted a persona to fit every situation? Are you the tough-as-nails jock on the mat, the gutter-mouthed sailor on poker night, and the pious and prayerful servant when it's expected?

It's true that every situation requires that certain forms be adhered to (certainly, you wouldn't start a line dance during a board meeting), but every one of us needs to examine the question of continuity of character. Your character is your foundation, the manifestation of your belief system. If you believe that your character changes with each situation, you're incorrect. Your performance only changes in an attempt to either enhance or conceal something that is deeply embedded.

Want to discover your true character? Consider your motivations for doing the right things. Are you performing, or simply being yourself?

You've seen the credits that roll at the end of a program. The regular actors are assigned characters to play…people who may or may not be similar to themselves. But once in a while, a big-name actor or actress makes a guest appearance and plays themselves – no fabricated name or persona. What role will you play?

> **"Be more concerned with your character than your reputation, because your character is what you really are, while your reputation is merely what others think you are."**
> **–John Wooden**

PROMOTE THE PROGRAM

Commitment for Advancement

You've heard the maxim, "All or Nothing." You've also heard, "When the Going Gets Tough, the Tough get Going." Here's what you can extract from both: if you're not going to get tough and give all of your resources (even in challenging times), then move on to something to which you can commit your whole self.

What does it mean when you sign your name to a membership document, a contract, or a pledge or petition? Is it simply an additional, theoretical association that you can add to your resume? Or does your signature or verbal commitment tie you to that organization with moral steadfastness and allegiance?

Roll up your real or proverbial sleeves. Arrive early to set up for the show; hand out programs; stay late to sweep the stage. Offer fresh ideas for raising funds; research past promotion successes; hit the streets and sell products. Volunteer to paint lines on the field; mentor a player; commit to extra practice time. Go to PTA meetings; be a classroom guest reader; come to career day to share your success story. Make customer service a personal priority; endeavor to increase sales; offer feedback at company meetings.

These are just a few examples of ways you can go above what's expected to promote the success of your organization. Even if you're an organization of one, commitment to your own success with diligence and a willingness to make yourself visible (in good times and bad) will hasten your realization of success.

"The irony of commitment is that it's deeply liberating – in work, in play, in love"

–Anne Morriss

RESPECT IS EARNED

Demands for
it Result
in Embargo

If you demand money, and receive it, you have money. If you demand respect, and receive it, you are being duped. Nothing as benevolent as respect could ever be taken by force. Instead, it must be secured with a patient hand that understands its nature.

Respect is interpersonal, acknowledges feelings, and is wrought with an investment of time and a demonstration of quiet strength. When you give it, you put out a welcome mat to receive it.

Imagine this: a business associate of yours takes very important matters seriously. She listens with intent. She practices self control, and is honest about her own abilities and her own mistakes. She uses clean and proper language, and is willing to not only admit what she doesn't know, but to go out and expand her mind by learning more.

Now this: a new man is hired to work in your office. He announces upon his arrival that he's one of the most competent people that could have been hired. He says that he always demands respect, and always gets it.

Which coworker gets your respect? Which person would you emulate in your quest for respect?

Consider respect something that must be gained with patience and a modest timeline – it can't be hurried, nor can its givers be strong-armed. Respect is not free, nor can it be purchased or stolen. It can only be gifted by and to its giver – in true demonstration of the circular Golden Rule.

"Men are respectable only as they respect"
–Ralph Waldo Emerson

SUCCESSFUL MENTORS ARE ACTIVE MENTEES

Recycle Foresight; Reduce Hindsight

As part of your everyday life, are you a:
A. teacher
B. student?

How about a:
A. guider
B. guided?

What about a:

A. mentor
B. mentee?

If you find yourself struggling, wishing for a choice *C* on all three questions, you would indisputably earn an "*A*" for yourself. None of us are one-directional information highways. We pass what we have learned to others – either deliberately or unintentionally.

The conscious awareness of the circular nature of learning is what sets good mentors apart from mediocre ones. A good teacher never stops learning; or gathering foresight from those who have already endured what lies ahead.

By converting another's hindsight to your foresight, you can pass that wisdom to your dependents, shaving sweat and tears from their personal goal achievement.

In order to be a better mentor, you must vow to never abandon your own learning, or your own admiration of those who inspire you. When you open yourself to learning from those who embody the realization of your personal aspirations, you multiply not only the benefits that you will realize, but also those that you are able to pass along to your own protégés. You become an electrically-charged conduit of knowledge.

Never stop learning. Never stop teaching. The latter cannot fully and robustly exist without the former.

"To be a good student takes as much wisdom as it does to be a good teacher"
–J.J. Dewey

IS IT TIME TO REINVENT YOURSELF?

Turning the Page to a New Chapter

Moving from one chapter in your life to the next doesn't require reincarnation, only reinvention. Reinvention is defined as the bringing back into existence something that has been neglected or obscure. Simply put, when you reinvent something, you bring forth a new version.

Life demands periodic reinvention. As we grow, we must reinvent ourselves from baby, to toddler, to adolescent, to teenager, to adult. When marriage and careers are chosen, commitment strengthens and transforms us once again. But often, the attitude is adopted that reinvention stops there – that changes only need to be made in response to requirement. Think again.

Knowledge and experience change perceptions of self and the world. When your perceptions change enough to make your current circumstance feel stagnant, it's time for self-reinvention.

When you sponsor a life of dormancy, you write a book without one of the most important components of a good story – change. If a story's character doesn't change, there's no story. If there are no plot twists, there's no reason to turn pages. If there are no notable differences in the main character from beginning to end, your book (or your life, in this case) gets poor reviews from its toughest critic – you.

Define what you want to be and become it; shed the parts of you that no longer fit. You've heard that there's no reason to reinvent the wheel. You're not a wheel, but you are no less than a rich-with-potential main character… in a novel just waiting to be written.

> **"You cannot change your destination overnight, but you can change your direction overnight."**
> **–*Jim Rohn***

THE DEFINITION OF INSANITY:

Do what you
Have Always done
and Expect
Different Results

This is your morning commute: you're cut off, you're forced to avoid one accident after another, you see the same disgruntled faces in the same dented cars every day. By mile seven, there's bottle-necking in anticipation of an upcoming merge. Around the fifteen mile on the freeway, you begin to wonder why it's called "free."

You begin each day at the office with a clenched jaw and flippant words for your coworkers. You try to think positively, but it takes time to calm your nerves.

Despite your frustration, you continue to believe that the "freeway" is the easiest and most efficient way to get from point A to point B. Because they say so. Who are "they?"

You are not insane, but your choices have led to behavior that mirrors insanity. You've chosen to bang your head against the steering wheel because humans are often held back from exploring options by fear, a perception that the current method is the easiest, and a lack of knowledge about options.

To make a change, you must think about past successes – how did behavior that affected past, positive change differ from other behaviors? Be flexible and open to new suggestions from those who can offer advice (and ask for that advice). You must be willing to experiment and to seek education.

To change your situation, you must examine your approach. Find an alternate route, carpool, or take the bus. Open your mind and you'll clear a new path to your destination.

> ## "Our solutions must be beyond anything we have ever considered,… We should not be afraid to try bold new approaches."
> ### *–Mary Landrieu*

IS YOUR GLASS HALF FULL?

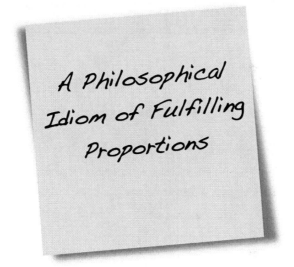

A Philosophical Idiom of Fulfilling Proportions

Rather than ask if your glass is half empty or half full, perhaps I should pose the question in this way: "Are you emptying your glass or filling your glass?"

When you view your glass (your life) as half-full, you increase the volume of its contents until it flows over to extinguish the burning, self-defeating thoughts of those who look to you for direction. In other words, your attitude will be contagious. Your positive outlook will prove to be irresistible to those with whom you work, live, and play.

Optimism is a choice. A positive outlook is not inherent to humans, nor is it a factor determined by genetics. It is not a response to living conditions, or a direct result of past experiences. Instead, it is the affirmation of good, in anticipation of more good.

A flourishing athlete is often distinguished by a willingness to persevere. Many endearing stories speak of athletes' risings from adversity, but what those stories don't always mention are the optimistic forces that triumphed early on in those athletes' lives; and that most of those positive forces were external…parents, coaches, teammates.

Perseverance is not possible without optimism. Without optimism, every loss, every strike-out is viewed as a failure – a step backward and away from a goal. Teaching optimism is the most foolproof and self-sufficient method for demonstrating triumph.

Victory isn't always illustrated on a score board, nor is it defined equally for all involved. Rather, victory is the decision to be a victor, not a victim. When you declare that your glass is half-full, you multiply your triumphs.

When you view your life-glass as half-full, you're not only pronouncing your optimism, but you're filling the glasses of those around you. Your attitude will brim, it will spill over, and it will flood others' spirits with the power to achieve.

"A pessimist is one who makes difficulties of his opportunities and an optimist is one who makes opportunities of his difficulties."
–Harry Truman

MISERY LOVES COMPANY, ALL OF THE TIME

You ARE What you Attract

By now, you might have grasped the power of positive thinking. But to check yourself, there is a test to determine exactly what kind of vibrations you're sending into the world. What kinds of people are drawn to you? Are they upbeat, forward-thinking, and optimistic? Or are they grumbling, miserable, negative thinkers? It's no secret – you are what you attract.

Watch people at a party, or a sporting event, or at the water cooler. Notice the demeanors of the groups…notice what they talk about, and how they view the world. Often, the grumblers will gang together to lament over the sad state of political matters or the cloudy weather; while the groups on the other end of the outlook spectrum will highlight the accomplishments of politicians whom they agree with, or will talk about the beautiful sunny weather.

To promote your own positive energy, choose friends and colleagues who are mutually positive. Miserable people naturally want to pull others down with them, so avoiding relationships with these people will lead to more uplifting and positive interactions.

If you find yourself attracting people that are more negative than you, try to focus on the ideals that you want for yourself, and your subconscious will guide you toward people that share those ideals.

You have the right and duty to guard what you allow to enter your own consciousness. When you surround yourself with positive people, you compound your own positive attraction for personal success. After all, happiness revels in company, too.

> ## "Life is partly what we make it, and partly what is made by the friends we choose."
> ### –*Tennessee Williams*

KEEP UP RATHER THAN CATCH UP

Better Yet, Stay Ahead

On your mark, get set, GO! Runners are pounding the track on either side of you. Your heart resounds in your chest cavity. As you round the second bend, the sweat begins to accumulate and run into your eyes. By the third, you consider falling back. You need a break. You could catch up if you just had a few seconds…

Assume for a moment that you and your fellow runners start the race at an average of 12 mph. Some runners fall behind, but you and the other top athletes maintain a steady gait for the first half of the race. When you consider backing off to take a break, you run the risk of falling eternally behind.

If you were to back off to 10 mph, you would have to run faster than even the fastest runner to catch up. If you were to slow to a walk, about 2.7 mph, you would be hard-pressed to catch up, even if you were capable of an NFL 22 mph or the top recorded human speed of 30 mph.

Catching up is possible, but the margin of success is infinitesimal. Falling behind is a choice with serious consequences; but if you make the conscious choice to keep up, you make a choice to reject the wasting of your time and energy in trying to catch up. When you commit to keeping up, you conserve that time and energy for moving forward – toward your goal.

There is a third, superior, option: hold yourself to a higher standard. Work harder. Start and finish the race at a steady 13 mph, and you'll not only stay ahead, you'll win.

"You get out in front – you stay out in front."
–A.J. Foyt

ALWAYS BELIEVE IN YOURSELF

Selective Memory
Builds Faith

Belief is a certainty in the truth of a proposition. When you believe in yourself, you confirm your ability to exist brilliantly.

We often believe in things without any proof – yet, we lose faith in what lies beneath the skin that we live in.

Few belief systems have the ring of truth like the belief in oneself. It's the only belief system in which the subject and object are both the biggest truth that one will ever have the opportunity to know – Self.

Self-efficacy is the belief that you have the power to generate a desired effect. It differs from self-esteem in that it doesn't measure self-worth, but personal ability. Individuals with high self-efficacy demonstrate planning skills, diligent work ethics, heartening with adversity, and self-control. Additionally, when you believe in your own abilities, you are less likely to become a victim of failure, and more likely to welcome it as the learning mechanism that it really is.

To boost your own self-efficacy, build your positive bank of episodic memories; in other words, fill your resume with success stories by achieving attainable goals. Find a paradigm; a self-believing person that you can model. Welcome positive feedback and commit it memory. And finally, know that your reactions to stress are not indicators of your ability to accomplish a task – they are simply reactions to stress.

Even amnesiac patients, after losing episodic memory, maintain their beliefs in self. It's really that deeply rooted.

Believe in you. Others will see your conviction and believe, too.

"Whether you think you can or you think you can't – you are right."
–Henry Ford

GET OUT OF YOUR COMFORT ZONE, NOW!

Stepping Out and Stepping Up

Everyone has comfort zones. Even highly motivated, successful people do; but they choose to regularly step outside of their enclosures.

In order to identify, and at least temporarily spurn, your own comfort zone, it's important to understand what a comfort zone is. It's a position that's relatively free from anxiety, and that uses restricted behaviors to elicit predictable results. Your comfort zone can be a place where you reside within the identity that your self image assigns to you. It can also be a result of what your habits and attitudes have taught you that you are.

Mental boundaries cause false senses of security. When these mental boundaries keep us in comfort zones (which are ruts, really), we rob ourselves of the ability to try new things and experience new successes – and that equals stagnancy.

When you make the conscious choice to step out of your comfort zone, your anxiety level is increased. As a result, your stress responses are heightened. As a benefit of these physiological responses, your concentration and your focus are sharpened, giving you the survival-rooted edge that's necessary for success.

Start with small steps out. You can run out and run back in, or you can make your short excursion an extended stay; the importance lies in confronting fear every time.

Cowering inside of a comfort zone is a common human response; but unless you want to remain a common human, you must take a trip outside that perceived security, and toward authentic success.

"Progress always involves risks. You can't steal second base and keep your foot on first."
–Frederick B. Wilcox

HABITS ARE THE BACKBONE OF GOOD AND BAD LUCK

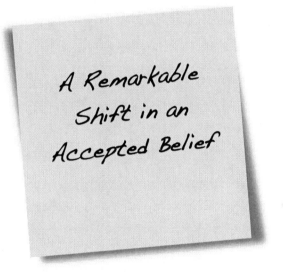

A Remarkable Shift in an Accepted Belief

Luck is a term assigned to episodes we can't explain. It doesn't exist. More appropriate words might be windfalls or disasters. But general good or bad luck? You might as well surrender control of your life and wait for the people with balloons and a giant check to ring your doorbell.

If you choose to change the direction of your general fortune, you'll need to invest in straightening your habit spine.

Habitual behaviors are results of learning, in which neural pathways are forged, resulting in subconscious, repetitive conduct. Often, we don't even recognize that we have a bad habit until someone points it out to us. Ask a nail-biter how many hours a day he spends assaulting his cuticles, and he'll grossly underestimate. Ask a procrastinator how often she puts off important tasks, and she'll say she'll get back to you.

Bad habits either divert you from the path that you intend to be on (smoking will hold you back from running the marathon), or consume the time that you need to spend on reaching goals (oversleeping will cut into your basketball training time, affecting your scholarship goal).

Good habits will wind through daily activities and further success: good study habits lead to good grades; arriving to work on time expands the chances for promotion.

Is the backbone of your prosperity straight and upright? Or is it twisted with the scoliosis of bad habits? Thoroughly examining your condition is the first step in curing the affliction known as "bad luck."

"Out of our beliefs are born deeds;
out of our deeds we form habits;
out of our habits grows our character;
and on our character we
build our destiny."
–Henry Hancock

TIME MANAGEMENT

First Things
First, and
Major in
the Majors

Time management is a misleading expression. No one can manage time. It manages itself, and marches on with no regard for our wanting more.

As with any challenge, it's important that you look internally to find an answer to an external problem. Time cannot be managed, but the way in which you manage your undertakings can.

How to find out what's most important? You can use task comparison,

---

in which you capture and compare pairs of tasks to determine which will most effectively further your cause. Or, you can concentrate on problems that need to be solved by tackling the tasks that will contribute to working out your biggest problems first.

You might want to consider profitability – tackle the tasks that will yield the biggest goal-reaching results first. And often, external pressure needs to be considered when prioritizing – if your boss, client, or coach establishes a timeline, you'll need to adopt the attitude of "first things first" in order to honor it.

The Law of the Vital Few maintains that 20 percent of your task list will yield 80 percent of your most valuable results. Isolate that 20 percent, so that you can protect your allotment of time like the valuable commodity that it is – or success will slip through your hands as steadily as the sands of time slip through the hourglass.

> ## "The key is not to prioritize what's on your schedule, but to schedule your priorities."
> ### *–Stephen R. Covey*

MEASURE WHAT MATTERS, AND WHAT MATTERS WILL ALWAYS IMPROVE

How Strategic Scrutiny Enriches your Best Assets

One of a parent's greatest wishes for their child might be sending that child to an Ivy League college. The first item of business for that parent will be to determine the most important factors for the realization of that goal.

Homework is a good place to start. Homework matters because it is a foundation upon which work ethic and good grades are based. When a parent asks, "Do you have any homework?" a child will learn, with guidance, that good performance in the homework arena will correlate to good test grades, which will result in consideration by the most prestigious institutions of higher learning.

In this example, homework is what matters. By determining what matters most to your success, you can more easily assess how you can improve it. When you honestly measure the efforts that you make, they will improve by default. When you measure what matters, you are essentially isolating those standards that are most crucial to your success and focusing on them.

What is left unmeasured will never get done; and conversely, what is measured will progress. Examine and fix only things that contribute to your life's cause – otherwise, you'll have made repairs, but those repairs will do nothing to contribute to your personal achievement.

Measure the matters that matter – and like plants or children, the matters that matter will flower beneath your thoughtful attention.

"Evaluate what you want – because what gets measured gets produced."
– *James A. Belasco*

TURN "IMPOSSIBLE" INTO "I'M POSSIBLE"; IT'S ALL A STATE OF MIND

How Simple Belief can Redefine Delusion

What can we learn from the unbridled ambition of children? Your answer may be only a remembrance away.

No one laughs or casts an expression of doubt or pity upon a child when he or she proclaims a wish to become a rock star, or a biophysicist, or a professional athlete, or an astronaut. No one discourages the pursuit of a law degree, or a doctorate, or a world record when a starry-eyed kid displays utter and unabashed belief in him or herself.

So why, as we grow and gain power over our own lives and the lives of others, do we lose faith in our personal ability? Why do we listen to the voices, both audible and muted, that tell us we're too old, washed up, or just not good enough? At what point do we lose our self-truth?

Often, folks with big dreams are tagged as delusional. What a paradox this is, considering that the only delusion in the pursuit of fulfillment is impossibility itself. For anyone to believe in impossibility, they would have to blatantly deny the state of the world that we live in.

How long ago was space travel considered to be impossible? Or cloning? Or internet connectivity? How many people laughed at Grandma Moses? Or Alexander Graham Bell?

It's time for you to discard the stale delusion of impossibility and to act; to adopt the limitless belief in possibility; and to recover your very own buried treasure of potential.

"You have powers you never dreamed of. You can do things you never thought you could do. There are no limitations in what you can do except the limitations of your own mind."
–Darwin P. Kingsley

CHALLENGE YOURSELF

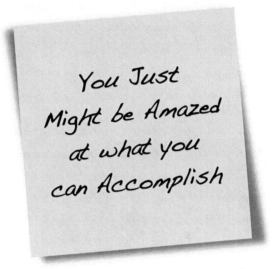

You Just Might be Amazed at what you can Accomplish

The Psychology of Resistance to Change asks that we stay in the safest place possible – which for most of us, continues to be in our current situation, conducting the tasks that we know are easily accomplished with reasonable success.

But, despite that intrinsic human tendency, individuals who break out of that comfort zone, to confront their fears and self-established limitations, tend to be the most successful.

Business moguls and Olympians were not born signing deals or jumping hurdles. Popular spiritual leaders and effective parents had to push boundaries to realize true success. They all learned that an attraction to healthy stress (pushing against a self-defined limit) delivered them to their peak performances, and that continued pushing resulted in a more astonishing outcome every time.

Go toward your fear. In order to fear, you must feel some desire for the thing that you fear. Maybe you're not afraid to ride a bull, because you may never have to do it. But you might fear public speaking – something you know is inevitable for the growth of your business. Push against that fear. It is a clear signal of where you must go.

No surprise is more appreciated than one initiated by self, and presented to self. Name your current limit, but never name your ultimate limit. The simple act of challenging yourself contributes more to your self-esteem than the outcome of that challenge; and knowing that you tried reinforces the idea that you are, indeed, limitless.

"Always do your best and your best gets better."
–Brett (Coach) Davenport

NEVER GIVE UP

Forging Ahead Tirelessly

Raising the white flag. *"I surrender."* *"You win."* These sentiments are only appropriate in cases involving gunfire or true love. No matter how you say it, *giving* in, *giving* out, or *giving* up is never an acceptable answer to any obstacle to success. If you want success, the only suitable response to impediment is to *"give* everything you've got."

Here are a few examples of people who have *given* it:

- Rodin, *The Thinker's* sculptor, was dubbed uneducable, an idiot, and was refused admittance to art school three times.

- Albert Einstein was considered to be mentally dim, was expelled from school, and had his PhD rejected.

- Margaret Mitchell's *Gone with the Wind* was turned down by twenty-five publishers.

- Beethoven handled a violin clumsily; was called a "hopeless composer."

- George Lucas' Star Wars was turned away from every Hollywood movie studio except one.

- Hershel Walker was told he was too small to be a running back.

- Walt Disney was terminated because he wasn't creative enough, and he declared bankruptcy numerous times.

- Fred Astaire was told he wasn't good at acting, and that his dancing ability was only marginal.

- Elvis Presley was fired by the Grand Ole Opry. He was told that he had no future, that he should drive a truck.

- Don't give up. Instead, give everything in you. The odds might not seem to be in your favor, but the biggest pay-offs always come from the highest odds.

"Every strike brings me closer to the next home run."
–Babe Ruth

OFTEN, LIFE'S MOST VALUABLE LESSONS ARE LEARNED FROM GOOD, OLD FASHIONED, HONEST EFFORT

Learn to Recognize "Easy" as a Limitation

There are some who say that work ethic has gone out with hoop skirts and handlebar mustaches. I disagree. The line at the counter just happens to be shorter.

Hard work is just that: it's work and it's hard. That's why the masses aren't lined up to participate. But a quick look into the benefits of a solid work ethic quickly makes it clear that this retroactive view is the best choice.

Few kids aspire to be a soccer goalie, so coaches often use rotation to fill the position. True, being a goalie is hard. You have to be alert. You are the team's last defense. There's pressure. You're alone, defending the seemingly undefendable. But the wise one sees opportunity in that position. Because the goalie spot requires distinctively difficult training, a successful goalie is often highlighted…pointed out… showcased in instant replays. The goalie is celebrated in a manner that underlines work ethic.

Human beings innately move away from pain. That's why many avoid hard work. But in paradox (where most valuable ideals are found), hard work results in pleasure. It builds character, challenges us to know ourselves as limitless, pushes us ahead of our competitors, and delivers unrivaled satisfaction. Once you experience the high of hard work, you'll be inclined to return, again and again.

When you invest effort, you become your own compelling force. You're no longer limited by "easy." Instead, your potential is immeasurable because you are willing to not simply walk, but to run, the extra mile.

"There are no traffic jams along the extra mile."
–Roger Staubach

COURAGE: WE ARE ONLY AS GOOD AS OUR WEAKEST LINK

Sometimes it Might be our Best Player, Manager, Producer...

In the 1939 musical, *The Wizard of Oz*, a group of travelers (Dorothy, Tin Man, Scarecrow, and Cowardly Lion) are on a journey to meet the Wizard of Oz, who can purportedly advise them on how to get home, get a heart, get a brain, and gain courage, respectively.

Surely, each character plays a part in hindering the journey, but the Cowardly Lion puts on quite a show with his perceived lack of courage. He holds up the group numerous times with his fear…often marking him as the weakest link.

Lions are the kings of their jungles by nature. Often, we assume our best players, managers, or producers to be kings or queens of their jungles, too. But without courage, any one of these entities falls flat.

The lion slowed down the whole group because he didn't realize that fear had nothing to do with cowardice. He thought that bravery meant the nonexistence of fear.

In reality, courage is the choice to take action, despite fear. In the situations in which the lion chose not to take action, he held up the group – they had to take the time to encourage him, to push him along the path. This didn't only slow down the lion's journey; it slowed down the journey of the entire group.

The lion's courage was there all along. Courage is not a lack of fear; it's the choice to confront that fear. When you embrace this, you hold the potential to be the strongest link.

"You gain strength, courage, and confidence by every experience in which you really stop to look fear in the face. You must do the thing which you think you cannot do."
–Eleanor Roosevelt

IT'S TRUE: ADVERSITY BUILDS CHARACTER

How to Find Fortune in Misfortune

Picture the person whom you most respect in this world. Has that person skated through life without too many bumps? Or has that person managed to weather the battering winds and floods of misfortune?

If this person is one of great character, it's likely that he or she has endured great adversity.

When faced with adversity, you have a choice. You can welcome it with a positive outlook, knowing that once the clouds have cleared, you will emerge as a stronger, more patient, and self-reliant person. Or, you can choose to run from it, fight it, deny it…until it happens nonetheless, hardening you against the life from which it comes.

Additionally, don't settle for overcoming adversity, but rather, push through it, to learn from it. Adversity is a mountain that springs up from the earth, along the path that you are traveling. You can climb over it (overcome). Or, you can cut your way through with a pick and an ax.

Though climbing that mountain will prove to be quite difficult, cutting through it will be even more painstaking. But the advantage of cutting through it is that when you return to the sight of that adversity – when you encounter hard times again – you will have forged a passage. You will enjoy a clear walking path.

There's no question; you will lose something in adversity. But if you accept adversity as a strengthening exercise, and focus on its benefits, you'll only trim the fat – nothing that you ever needed anyway.

"Smooth seas do not make skillful sailors."
–African Proverb

ENVY HOLDS BACK EVEN THE STRONGEST WILL

Defeating the Emerald Monster

Envy is a disease. Like a choking vine, envy slinks, almost undetectably, into a psyche. It may first be disguised as admiration, but when fed by a substance that leaks from a perforated self-esteem, it grows stronger, winding around values, ambition…and worst of all, the energy that we need for traveling through our own, very personal, journeys.

When you measure yourself against another whom you view as superior, either based on their talents, their opportunities, or their possessions, you threaten your own self-image. If your self-esteem has already been battered, you run an even higher risk of battering your will into submission.

One of the Seven Deadly Sins, envy holds a poisonous power to smash potential. When you focus on the "haves" of someone else, and wish you could have them for yourself, you automatically highlight your own shortcomings. You shift focus from your assets to your weaknesses, adopt a negative attitude…and it's all downhill from there.

It's important to recognize that we're all gifted with strengths, and that no two of us possesses the same combination, or the same intensities, of those gifts. Know that you're unique, and could not be just like anyone else – even if you spent your whole life trying.

You cannot be everything that someone else is, nor should you want to be. When you focus on another's efforts, you turn your own lens out of focus. You waste valuable time obsessing, when you could be working to achieve success that is uniquely *you*.

> ## "Keep yourselves far from envy; it eateth and taketh away good actions, like as fire eateth up and burneth wood."
> ### –*Muhammad*

LOVE GENEROUSLY, PRAISE LOUDLY, LIVE FULLY

The idea that praise can be damaging, by creating over-inflated egos, has gone out with the top hat. It's clear that when we love unconditionally and praise appropriately, the receivers of those endowments grow to be confident, motivated, and ready to take on challenges.

Sincere praise takes practice. The way that you praise others will determine how well it is received, as well as the "take away" factors of that praise.

Be spontaneous. Choose moments of praise wisely. Random praise will establish trust in your words.

Isolate performance. Compare an individual's performance to his or her own past performances, and note improvement. It's important to teach personal mastery, not competition with peers.

Be sincere and specific. When you praise honestly and without motive, and praise precise characteristics of an accomplishment, you build confidence in the receiver.

Praise for hard work. When praise is delivered for execution that is a result of work ethic, and not natural ability, you encourage future effort.

Always leave room for improvement. By avoiding words like "best ever," you keep standards for enhancement within reach.

Love and praise are circular contributions. To get love, give love. To create positivism, be positive and supportive. And to live fully, enrich the lives of everyone who is fortunate enough to know you with love and praise.

"Praise is like sunlight to the human spirit: we cannot flower and grow without it."

–Jess Lair

BE PREPARED

Today Might
Hold your
Opportunity

A football running back (a high school sophomore) displays many of the attributes that it takes to be great: quick feet, foresight, and explosive speed. There are areas that he knows need improvement (like his consistency, for example), but he knows he has another year or two until he needs to decide where he'll play college ball, and to be concerned about talent scouts hiding along the sidelines.

This boy couldn't be more wrong. Opportunity is stealthy. It appears without warning, and shows no mercy for ill-prepared candidates.

If opportunity could be orchestrated, the boy would first decide which college he'd like to play ball for, and scouts would schedule appearances for specific games, in which they would eat hotdogs from the stands while holding "scout" flags high above the crowd.

Many opportunities are lost due to being unprepared. Often, we adopt the thinking that once we're prepared, then we can start waiting for opportunities to arise. The truth is that when opportunity appears, if you can't prove immediately that you've done the work to excel, and that you have more good ideas and projects over the fire, that opportunity will prove to be only a chance meeting with disappointment.

There's too much competition among scouting organizations to waste time on a player who doesn't demonstrate optimum ability and commitment. Unfortunately for the football player, he'll never know that he was observed, but cast off. He'll assume that opportunity never presented itself – when in reality, he never presented himself.

"It wasn't raining when Noah built the ark."

–Howard Ruff

TOGETHER EVERYONE ACHIEVES MORE...

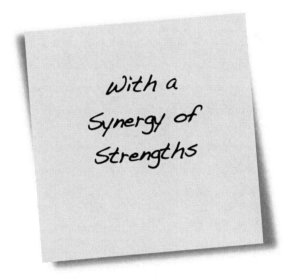

With a Synergy of Strengths

You've heard that the whole is greater than the sums of its parts. That's a good place to start when speaking about teams, but at the same time, it robs a well-constructed team of the credit that it deserves.

Successful team builders know that a group does not make a team. A group may cooperate with one another, but only a true team collaborates. Team members are accountable to one another, as well as to the greater purpose. The decisions made are wiser, more thought out, and better than any single-minded decision could ever claim to be. Resources are multiplied when the strengths of each team member is developed and utilized.

When teams are established (sports, work, school, music, family), more is accomplished than any one person could ever achieve. When talents and skills are collaborated, people are empowered because they are now privy to external strengths that compensate for their own perceived weaknesses.

When individuals feel support and trust, they naturally share knowledge freely. They feel multiplied fulfillment – both as individuals, and as part of an alliance. Empowerment is felt, complex tasks are accomplished, and lofty goals are realized.

Flour alone cannot feed a family. Neither can yeast, salt, nor water. But when all are maximized for their strengths, individuals, families, and communities are nourished.

That's how an effective team works. It maximizes the complementary strengths, and minimizes the weaknesses, of its constituents…so that together, everyone can achieve more.

"Individual commitment to a group effort – that is what makes a team work, a company work, a society work, a civilization work."
–Vince Lombardi

THE CHALLENGE OF CHANGE

Change: A Potent Concoction of Success Stimulants

When you're asked to change, what's your first reaction? Human nature would dictate that you resist that change, particularly if you are comfortable in your current situation. Even if your current situation isn't ideal, sometimes the concept of change incites resistance – even among the bravest of souls.

This resistance is nothing new. When ancient peoples roamed the earth, moving to new locations was only embraced when their current living situations proved to be unbearable – either they'd run out of food, or wild animals were taking too many lives, or invading tribes threatened their safety.

In much the same way, we're often reluctant to take on change unless we're pushed to do so. But, if you can learn to seek out change as an option instead of a last resort, to embrace it, and to know that the benefits that lie at the end of the winding road are invaluable, you will advance beyond your greatest expectations.

The challenge of change is recognizing that everything you fear is necessary for success.

- When you step out of routine or habitual behavior, you compound your chances for opening avenues for success.

- When you abandon the residual feelings from bad past change experiences, you free yourself to look only forward.

- When you move beyond your insecurity and toward anxiety and stress, you boost your productivity quotient.

- When you shed your fear of loss, you can take on the anticipation of gain.

There's no arguing that change is difficult, particularly when it's imposed by an outside source, but there's also no arguing with the power of change. Change has the power to change your life – for the better.

> "It takes a lot of courage to release the familiar and seemingly secure, to embrace the new. But there is no real security in what is no longer meaningful. There is more security in the adventurous and exciting, for in movement there is life, and in change there is power."
>
> –*Alan Cohen*

SMILE AND LAUGH OFTEN – BOTH ARE INCREDIBLY HEALTHFUL

This Prescription Really Could be the Best Medicine

Smiles are indispensable in our personal, business, and recreational lives. When you smile, others want to know what's so great. They can't help but smile back because biology dictates that their brains activate the facial muscles that will return your upturned offering.

Try it. The next time someone smiles, try to frown. Or try to smile while thinking a negative thought. A smile is a window into a soul; and possibly more interestingly, it also serves as a door to better health.

A simple smile relieves stress, releases endorphins and serotonin, lowers blood pressure, and boosts immunity.

Even better than a smile? Laughter. Did you know that one minute of laughing can raise your heart rate to the same level as if you spent ten minutes doing aerobic exercise? Or that fifteen minutes of laughing can burn up to fifty calories? Not only that, but laughing stretches facial and bodily muscles. It increases pulse and breathing, delivering more oxygen to organs and tissue. It promotes proper blood vessel contractions, it increases antibodies and the production of healthy cells, it lowers blood sugar, it reduces pain, and it promotes deeper sleep.

It's important to understand that neither smiles nor laughter are solely responsible for any of the social or health benefits that they offer. They're both outward manifestations of inner attitudes.

A face cannot smile if a heart is not enthusiastic. Find an upbeat mind-set, and you will find your upturned friend.

> ## "At the height of laughter, the universe is flung into a kaleidoscope of new possibilities."
> *–Jean Houston*

WHY IS 1/1/EVERYYEAR THE TIME WE START TO GET COMMITTED?

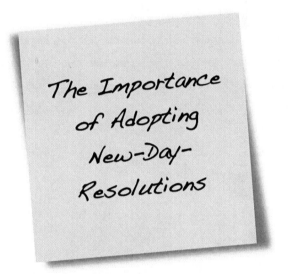

The Importance of Adopting New-Day-Resolutions

You want to accomplish something – win a scholarship, beat your best time, clear time to take a protégé under your wing. But stop… push that goal to the back of your mind, because you're going to have to wait until January 1st for the undertaking.

As counterintuitive as that plan sounds, that's how counterproductive most resolutions are — particularly those made in response to traditional, mindless stimuli.

When the ball drops, signifying the start of a new year, many of us feel obligated to name something we're going to change about ourselves. And the problem with most of these resolutions is that they're under-developed, spontaneously announced goals, which if successfully realized, will take something away that our subconscious has already named as important to us.

Instead, I'd like to propose that when your inner and external motivators drive you to add, to enhance, to complement the person that you already are...take the first step toward that ambition immediately. It doesn't matter if it's January 1st or July 1st; midnight or noon. If your resolution, or commitment, is aligned with your value system (if it is of utter importance to you), waste not another moment in preparation for your fulfillment, or your ability to give copiously from that fulfillment.

Waste not this minute, and you shall want not for what has slipped away.

"Everything has a day one, start yours today."
—Brett (Coach) Davenport

www.bmdleadershipinstitute.com

IF YOU WANT SOMEONE TO HEAR YOU, WHISPER

Why the
Softly Spoken
is the
Best Received

Whether you're raising kids or raising money for the furthering of your professional success, raising your voice will never trigger intense listening.

Conduct your own experiment in audience reception. Your audience can consist of one person, or an entire auditorium. First, shout

---

instructions in their direction. Watch their faces as you deliver your rant. They might draw away with wide eyes, or cower under the weight of your volume. They might not absorb your words because they're too shocked at your outburst.

Now, whisper different instructions, just loud enough for them to hear. You'll notice that each listener leans in, squints in an effort to focus on your words. They might take on the thoughtful expressions of people who have been asked to be involved…because they have.

When you whisper, you share information that is perceived as cherished and special. Your listeners feel that they have been gifted with a bit of top secret, precious knowledge. They also feel that they are trusted – that you consider them worthy of protecting the information.

Just as no one shouts privileged information across a parking lot, no one shouts information that is imperative to the success of themselves or their team.

Listeners become conditioned to yelling. If a child or student hears you shout daily, that shout will lose its power. It will no longer be shocking, or attention-getting…it will only cause the blinds to close and the doors to slam shut.

Open their ears and open their minds…with a whisper.

> ## "A whisper can be stronger, as an atom is stronger, than a whole mountain."
> ### –Earl Wilson

ARE YOU PART OF THE PROBLEM OR THE SOLUTION?

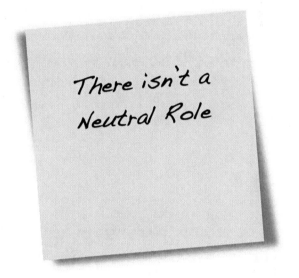

There isn't a Neutral Role

Imagine that you are an oarsman on a galley, or medieval ship, during the 8th century B.C. The rowing rhythm is counted out. The master strolls up and down the center of the rowing men. When his back is turned to you, you continue with your forward-rowing motion, but raise your oar out of the water so that you won't have to work so hard.

When the master turns in your direction, you lower your oar back into the water and row.

You might not be doing everything you can to propel the ship toward the battle that will bring your nation victory, but you're also not as bad as some of the other oarsmen, who when the master's back is turned, push their oars into the water in and effort to slow the ship, causing chaos amid the other cadenced oars. These men are fearful of war and are doing what they can to delay arrival at the battle site.

In this scenario, you might believe that you are assuming a neutral role – that by coasting along, you are neither directly helping nor harming the common cause. Here's the problem with that theory: if you're not part of the solution, you're part of the problem. Unless you're making an effort, by adopting an attitude that will enact positive change and propel you toward your goal, you are an inhibitor.

There's only one way to be part of the solution – put your oar in the water and Row!

"The minute you shift to neutral when you're trying to go up a hill, you start going backwards."
–Anonymous

TAKE RESPONSIBILITY FOR YOUR ACTIONS

Make Solitaire the only Acceptable Blame Game

When a mistake is made, it cannot be undone. However, it's important to realize that you have the power to amend perceptions – with your reaction to the mistake's consequences.

When you take responsibility for your actions, and accept the consequences with decency, you send a powerful message to every person that your actions affected. Others know that you care about the impact you've created. They know that you're honest – that you're not likely to cover up mistakes in the future. They know that you hold yourself to a high, leadership-level standard, and they can confidently predict that the work you do will also reach that standard. When you take responsibility, others feel confident in assigning responsibility to you.

Maybe more than one party is guilty of botching an undertaking. When you stand up and take responsibility for your part in the debacle, you transform yourself into a bright neon sign that blinks things like *honesty*, *uprightness*, and *character*.

If you place blame for bad judgment on external factors, you shut off the energy supply that is needed for change. Improvement will never be desired by anyone who skates along, believing that exuding a façade of perfection is more important than dealing effectively with consequences.

When you take responsibility for your actions, you can move forward with fluidity. The weight, or guilt, that you bear will be lifted, and you'll be free to enact the change that will set you apart.

> ## "When you point your finger at someone or something, ironically three fingers are pointing back at you."
> *–Brett (Coach) Davenport*

LEADERSHIP IS SPECIAL

The Good News is that it can be Taught

Having strong convictions does not make a leader; speaking loudly for those convictions does.

Having a strong voice does not make a leader; having the convictions to fill out those words does.

Leadership is special because it is a dual gift. Part of the gift is having the moxie that it takes to speak out and to guide. The other part of the gift is being privy to knowledge that a good leadership mentor or parent can offer. Too often, people with the conviction to be effective leaders haven't been given the freedom, the permission, or the skills to lead.

We often hear that children are our future. This gets special consideration when speaking about molding leaders. If our children are not given the opportunity to practice their leadership abilities (and soon), our world might continue waiting for chiefs to materialize mysteriously from the woodwork. Are you willing to take that gamble?

Future leaders should be invited to give input and opinions, teach others what they know, observe goal-setting and goal-achieving, take on responsibility, create something, make decisions, take charge to figure out solutions, mimic the courage of a mentor, express convictions, help peers, and think positively.

Whether you're a leader-in-training or training a leader, it's important to recognize that good leaders own their principles and demonstrate their convictions with fervor. No one is a born-leader. But there are those who are born to *become* leaders, with the help of those who have led before them.

> ## "Any coward can fire someone; it takes a leader to recognize potential that has been misdirected and take them to the top."
> *–Brett (Coach) Davenport*

DON'T LOOK BACK, PLAN AHEAD

The Past has Passed

Imagine that you've bowled over a traffic cone with your car, and you can see the crumpled orange implement causing havoc on the highway behind you. Cars are swerving to avoid a chain reaction accident. Road crew workers are waving their arms. You can't keep your eyes on the road ahead because you're too busy gawking into

---

your rearview mirror. If another obstruction should fall into your path, you'll make the same mistake again – or worse.

Often, when you make mistakes, or others hurt you, you have an almost irresistible urge to dwell upon those negative happenings. The feelings that you felt in the past persevere, infuse negativity into your present, and darken the lens through which you view the future.

When you look to your past with anger or regret, your future is crippled. Shifting focus from past negative feelings and lending focus to the future is the first step to moving forward. As you "drive" through life, you must use peripheral vision to stay alert to your present – the views out your side windows. However, your primary focus, your forward sight, must be directed out your windshield – straight ahead, to your future.

To overwrite past negative feelings, you must immerse yourself in the things that will deliver you to the future that you dream about. Rip off the rearview mirror. Make sure your windows and windshield are clear, so that you can optimize your visibility for the winding road that lies ahead.

> ## "Change is the law of life. And those who look only to the past or present are certain to miss the future."
> ### –John F. Kennedy

COACH DAVENPORT'S 4-STEP PROCESS FOR EFFECTIVE GOAL SETTING

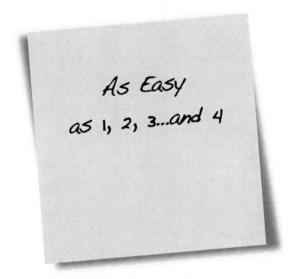

As Easy as 1, 2, 3...and 4

To give your life direction and to accomplish more, you'll need a plan for setting meaningful goals.

Follow my strategy for turning those elusive dreams into real, achievable goals, and you'll find your wishes for your life to be more attainable.

- Step 1: Set aside time for reflection. Write your dreams and goals onto paper. Hold nothing back – there are no limitations to your power, so there should be no limitations to your dreams.

- Step 2: Pick your top three goals. Concentrating on your most important goals will help to ensure that they get the attention they deserve (and that you'll get the success you deserve).

- Step 3: Create a vision board. Paste photos, clippings, words, phrases, or other visual examples, along with your three goals, onto poster board. All items should be examples of what you see for yourself once your goals are realized.

- Step 4: Recite your goals out loud, three times per day. Become accustomed to how your ideal success sounds. Listen to the words, allow them to guide your daily actions, understand that every time you recite them, they become a bigger part of your motivation toward success.

When you make your goals concrete parts of your life, you will have little choice but to follow the paths that they forge for you. Be answerable to your goals with these four steps, and you'll be on your way to transforming each one to reality.

"A goal properly set is halfway reached."

–Abraham Lincoln

WHAT IT TAKES
TO BE #1

*A Review
in the Success
of You*

Only you know what your ideal #1 is. Is it to make the most money? Or to be the most highly respected professional in your field? In your country? In the world? Does it mean being #1 in the eyes of your kids, or your students? Or does it mean that *you'll* know you're #1 because you've impressed your toughest critic?

We can't all take first place – there just aren't enough blue ribbons to go around. But what you can do is define what #1 means to you and focus on that prize.

In order to be #1, you must be willing to surrender something you might love, or lean on; you have to make sacrifices. You must be willing to remain loyal to your cause, even if it seems that your cause is the most difficult cause to be part of. You must be willing to execute the actions necessary for success.

If you want to achieve the status of #1, your attitude must earn an A+. Remain positive and refrain from falling into traps where deceitful behavior is acceptable. Hold yourself to a high standard, so that you can call yourself worthy of the #1 spot.

Know that difficulty will fortify you for the battles, as well as the successes, that lie ahead.

Refer to the previous 49 tips contained within this book, and know that your personalized formula lies within these offerings of wisdom…just as your personal success lies in your deepest treasure of resources – yourself.

> ## "The quality of a person's life is in direct proportion to their commitment to excellence, regardless of their chosen field of endeavor."
> ### –Vince Lombardi

REFERENCES AND SOURCES

Tip #4 – What you do Speaks so Loudly, I can't Hear What you Say
93% of communication is nonverbal. Tonya Reiman, *The Power of Body Language*, 2007, New York

Tip #25 – Keep up Rather than Catch up
The world record and Olympic record for human speed, 30 mph, was set by Asafa Powell, a Jamaican sprinter at the 2008 Beijing Summer Olympic Games.
http://en.wikipedia.org/wiki/Asafa_Powell

Reggie Bush, New Orleans Saints' running back, was clocked at 22 mph by ESPN on a punt return during the 2008 match-up with The Minnesota Vikings.
Sam Farmer, *Los Angeles Times*, October 12, 2008
http://articles.latimes.com/2008/oct/12/sports/sp-nfllines12

Tip #29 – Time Management
"The Law of the Vital Few" (a.k.a. The Principle Factor of Sparcity, 80-20 Rule, and the Pareto Principle), as defined in 1941 by management consultant Joseph M. Juran, in observance of the theories of Italian economist Vilfredo Pareto.
http://en.wikipedia.org/wiki/Pareto_principle

Tip #33 – Never Give up
Examples provided by Jack Canfield, Mark Victor Hansen, Bud Gardner, *Chicken Soup for the Writer's Soul*, 2000, Deerfield Beach, FL; and Mark Victor Hansen, Barry Spilchuk, Jack Canfield, *A Cup of Chicken Soup for the Soul*, 1996, Deerfield Beach, FL.

Tip #37 – Envy Holds Back Even the Strongest Will
Envy is established as one of the seven cardinal sins (worst vices for cutting a person from God's grace) of the Roman Catholic Church. St. Gregory the Great, *Moralia on Job*, 6th Century C.E.
http://www.newworldencyclopedia.org/entry/Seven_Deadly_Sins

NOTES

_____

_____

_____

_____

_____

_____

_____

_____

_____

_____

"I visualized where I wanted to be,
what kind of player I wanted to
become. I knew exactly where I
wanted to go, and I focused on
getting there."

–*Michael Jordon*

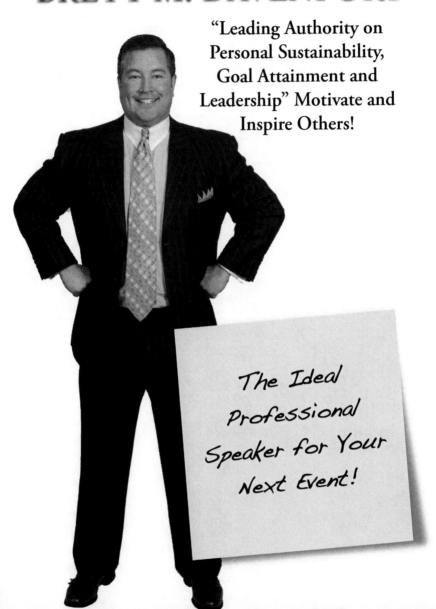

BRETT M. DAVENPORT

"Leading Authority on Personal Sustainability, Goal Attainment and Leadership" Motivate and Inspire Others!

The Ideal Professional Speaker for Your Next Event!

To Schedule Brett To Speak at Your Event:
Call: 1-888-5-YES U CAN · Visit: www.bmdleadershipinstitute.com
or Email: info@bmdleadershipinstitute.com

"SHARE THIS BOOK"

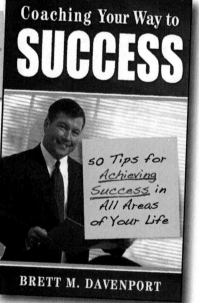

Coaching Your Way to

SUCCESS

50 Tips for _Achieving_ _Success_ in All Areas of Your Life

BRETT M. DAVENPORT